Original title:
Puns from the Pine Grove

Copyright © 2025 Creative Arts Management OÜ
All rights reserved.

Author: Vivienne Beaumont
ISBN HARDBACK: 978-1-80567-319-4
ISBN PAPERBACK: 978-1-80567-618-8

Laughter Leaves a Mark

In the grove where jesters play,
Laughter echoes, bright as day.
With every poke, a giggle's born,
Tickling ferns at early dawn.

Squirrels chuckle, acorns drop,
When branches sway, they simply flop.
A silly dance, the trees agree,
Nature's jesters, wild and free.

Folly in the Fir Boughs

The firs conspire to prank the sun,
With shadows sharp, it's all in fun.
A barky joke that rings quite true,
They shade the ground for a giggle or two.

Branches waving, a leafy cheer,
Whispers float, there's laughter near.
In every rustle, a secret shared,
Mirth in the air, none have a care.

The Witty Woodsman's Diary

In the pages of his trusty tome,
A woodsman writes from his forest home.
"Today I tripped on a branch's tease,
And fell right into a pile of leaves."

His quill drips jokes, a playful art,
Each entry crafted to warm the heart.
A bearded sage with a wink so sly,
He laughs with the owls, under the sky.

Shade-Side Shenanigans

Under the trees, where shadows dance,
    Critters plot their merry prance.
  A game of hide and seek they play,
With giggles echoing, come what may.

    A rabbit's leap, a squirrel's spin,
      Every twist, a chuckle begins.
  In shade and light, the fun won't cease,
In the heart of the grove, laughter's peace.

Forest Frolics of the Foliage

In the woods where creatures play,
Branches sway without delay.
Squirrels dance on a splintered log,
As shadows tease the morning fog.

Acorns drop like tiny bombs,
Filling the air with nutty charms.
A deer trips over a mossy stone,
Laughing loudly, never alone.

Laughing in the Leaf Litter

Leaves crunch loudly underfoot,
Nature's joke, a playful hoot.
A rabbit wiggles, tails in a knot,
Hiding treasures in a funny spot.

Beneath the boughs, a critter plays,
Hiding secrets in leafy bays.
Chirps and caws fill the air,
As laughter dances without a care.

Tipsy Trees and Chuckling Ferns

Tall trees sway, tipsy with glee,
Bending low for all to see.
Ferns giggle, their fronds a-flutter,
Whispering secrets in the mutter.

Gnarled roots twist in cheerful fright,
As shadows morph in playful light.
Barking at squirrels, the old oak grins,
Life's a jest where the fun begins.

Peculiar Pine Patter

Pine needles tickle as they fall,
Softly patting nature's hall.
A woodpecker raps a silly beat,
While rabbits hop and take a seat.

A fox winks with a knowing glance,
Inviting all to join the dance.
With every rustle, the forest sings,
In this grove of quirky things.

Treetop Tall Tales

In the branches high, tales entwine,
Squirrels share secrets, oh so divine.
A robin chirps songs that tickle the leaf,
While shadows chuckle, mocking belief.

The acorns drop with a thud and a grin,
Who knew such humor could dwell within?
Each rustle and whisper, a playful jest,
Nature's own laughter, forever blessed.

The Wooded Wordsmith's Whimsy

In the grove where stories grow and spin,
Trees whisper rhymes with a cheeky grin.
The woeful willow wishes for more,
While the clever creek spills jokes galore.

Each leaf a letter, each twig a word,
While the playful breeze sings what's unheard.
Nature pens scripts with delightful flair,
In this leafy stage, laughter fills the air.

Engaging Echoes of Enchantment

Echoes bounce off the trunks so grand,
Twisted tales told by the forest band.
The fox prances in with a tail of glee,
While rabbits giggle under an oak's spree.

Mice throw a party, cheese galore,
As owls hoot puns that make spirits soar.
Every rustling leaf is a pun on the breeze,
Nature's own laughter brings all to their knees.

Jesting in the Jungle Gym of Nature

In the boughs above, the humor swings,
As playful monkeys tie up their strings.
The vines are tight, but laughter escapes,
In this jungle gym, joy often shapes.

The parrots squawk with a vibrant cheer,
Making puns fly as they hop near.
With each silly blunder, the trees seem to sway,
In this natural circus, fun reigns the day.

Branching Out Into Laughter

In the grove, where jokes do sprout,
The branches bend with hearty clout.
Leaves chuckle softly, a rustling cheer,
As squirrels share tales that tickle the ear.

Bark's not just tough, it's punny too,
Each creak a quip that feels brand new.
Roots hold the secrets of jest so grand,
While vines entwine like a jesting band.

Sunlight filters with a playful wink,
While acorns exchange their quirky link.
The trees all sway, a humorous dance,
In this woodland realm, where laughter prance.

Come gather 'round, let the giggles bloom,
A forest symphony, dispelling gloom.
In every whisper, a pun takes flight,
Branching out together, in sheer delight.

Foliage of Fun and Folly

Under the leaves, where humor hides,
The foliage sways as laughter glides.
A berry's blush, a fruity jest,
Each petal whispers, we are blessed.

Saplings giggle, the older trees laugh,
Trunk to trunk, they share their craft.
Shade provides a comfy seat,
Where roots and jokes tend to meet.

In this realm of leafy cheer,
Nature's puns bring us near.
Dewdrops sparkle with witty light,
Creating smiles that feel just right.

As fall approaches, the colors change,
The pines stay green, but jokes rearrange.
In a world where mirth will always grow,
Foliage of fun, forever in tow.

Understory of Chuckles

In the understory, where tales unfold,
Small creatures gather with spirits bold.
Underbrush brimming with giggles sweet,
As laughter and leaves make quite the treat.

A rabbit hops, with a punny flair,
While shadows bring secrets that hang in the air.
The daisies nod, with such dainty grace,
As the breeze tickles, a warm embrace.

Beneath the canopy, smiles abound,
In this joyful haven, mirth is found.
A mischievous crow calls out in jest,
His feathers ruffle, he's simply the best.

So join the frolic, let humor sway,
In this playful spot, we'll laugh and play.
An understory rich with joyful sound,
Where chuckles echo, forever resound.

Allusions Among the Arboreal

In arboreal heights, humor takes flight,
Branches whisper, 'Let's lighten the night.'
With every breeze, a punchline flows,
As trees exchange quips and share their prose.

Maple giggles, while oak just grins,
The birch cracks jokes as the twilight begins.
Under the boughs, the laughter streams,
A canopy rich with whimsical themes.

Creeping vines weave tales so sly,
As leaves partake in a comical fly.
In the boughs above, wise owls decree,
'Nature's a joke, come laugh with me!'

So stay a while beneath lush green,
Where every moment is lively and keen.
Among the arboreal, we find our cheer,
In a grove where allusions bring us near.

Needle-nose Banter

In the grove where needles chat,
Trees gossip about this and that.
Spruce jokes are pointed, yet quite witty,
Laughter echoes, it's really quite nitty.

Fir friends share tales of outlandish sights,
With belly laughs under starry nights.
Watch out for pines with a sharp sense of fun,
They're always ready to pun and run!

Hilarity Under the Canopy

Beneath the branches, the laughter flows,
Bark jokes sprouting like wee little bows.
　Where shade provides a cool retreat,
　Tree trunks shimmy to a merry beat.

Hushed whispers in the leafy recess,
　Sharing tales of arborous excess.
Giggles rustle through the crisp, fresh air,
　It's fun to hear trees joke without a care.

Giggling Glades

In the glades where sunlight beams,
The trees are filled with snickers and schemes.
Every leaf holds a chuckle inside,
With each breeze, a new pun does glide.

Old oaks tease the saplings so spry,
While maples wave as if to fly.
Nature's humor is evergreen,
In giggling glades, joy's always seen.

The Jolly Juniper

Underneath the jolly juniper's sway,
Wise cracks make all the woes decay.
Its branches dance with quips and cheer,
A funny sight that draws us near.

With needle-sharp wit, it shares its lore,
As roly-poly critters roll on the floor.
Every rustle tells a snappy joke,
In the shade of this jovial oak!

The Bough Brochure of Banter

In the grove, the branches sway,
Leaves whisper jokes, come what may.
The squirrels chuckle, tails held high,
As acorns fall from the laughing sky.

A twig says, "I'm not a stick, I'm a limb!"
The trees all giggle, some laugh on a whim.
Their roots entwined in a playful jest,
Nature's humor, simply the best.

Chipmunk Chuckles and Chip Shots

Chipmunks dart with cheeky grins,
In a game of tags, they're all in.
Catching seeds, they share a grin,
A comic scene, no chance of din.

One says, "I'm nuts about this day!"
While dodging acorns that come to play.
The laughter spreads, it's quite a show,
With whiskers twitching, they steal the show.

The Stump's Secret Shtick

A old stump rests, it knows a lot,
With tales of trees and seeds they've caught.
It whispers secrets, a gnarled grin,
Of squirrels' antics and where they've been.

"Did you hear? The bark is worse than bite!"
The stump cackles, oh what a sight!
With tales of lumber that lumbered too,
Spreading laughter amidst the dew.

Breezy Banter in the Boughs

Winds carry chuckles through the trees,
Whistling jokes with a gentle breeze.
"Why did the pine never get lost?"
"Because it knows the way at any cost!"

Branches sway, in rhythm they sway,
Tickled leaves dance, come what may.
Nature's humor, in cozy embrace,
A cheerful chorus in this leafy space.

Laughter Between the Leaves

When squirrels debate on the best acorn,
They crack each other up till the morn.
A branch dangles low, wearing a face,
And whispers, "I'm stumped, oh what a place!"

The owls crack wise with a hoot or two,
Their wisdom is funny, you know it's true.
A deer rides a tree like a classic old car,
While giggling at jokes from a nearby star.

Roots of Riddle and Rhyme

Down in the dirt, where the creatures play,
The rabbits tell tales that always sway.
With roots intertwining, they spin a yarn,
About carrots that dance in the cool sweet dawn.

The woodpecker taps to a rhythmic beat,
As mushrooms crack jokes while trying to tweet.
They giggle at gnomes who think they are spry,
While plotting a prank on the clouds up high.

Hilarity in the Hollow

In a hollow so snug, the critters convene,
With laughter so loud, it's simply obscene.
A hedgehog plays tricks, with his spiny disguise,
While the rabbits all chuckle, their laughter won't die.

The turtles are slow, but their jokes are not,
They relish the moments, giving quite a shot.
With every old saying that they dig up,
The roots laugh along while they all share a cup.

Giggles in the Glade

In the glade where the sunbeams tickle the ground,
The flowers are laughing, a soft, silly sound.
A butterfly flutters, slips on a breeze,
And giggles with bees, making everyone sneeze.

Beneath the tall pines where the shadows play,
Frogs croak out jokes that just slay all day.
The crickets chirp puns from dusk until dawn,
While the fireflies flicker like lights on a lawn.

Evergreen Chuckles

In the forest, a tree took a stand,
Said, "I'm rooting for you, isn't it grand?"
A squirrel replied with a nut in tow,
"I can't help but crack up, don't you know?"

With branches that sway and leaves that hum,
They shared giggles under the sun's warm drum.
A pine cone dropped with a plop and a thud,
"Looks like we've got a pine-sational dud!"

Whispers of the Wooded Wordplay

Amid the tall trees where laughter grows,
A wise old owl had jokes, I suppose.
He hooted and hollered, made all the peeps,
"Why did the tree bring a ladder? For sheeps!"

The frogs in the pond joined in with glee,
"Why did the beetle break up with the bee?"
The answer was sweet, like honey, indeed,
"He found her too buzz-y, just took the lead!"

Cones of Jest and Joy

Underneath the canopy, shadows play,
A chipmunk danced, all ready to sway.
"I'm nuts about this party, can't you tell?"
With every step, he rang his bell.

The birch trees whispered with each gentle breeze,
"Why strive to grow up? Just try to appease!"
A fox in the thicket played hide and seek,
"I'm in a foxy mood; let's let laughter speak!"

Timbered Twists of Tickle

The forest floor erupted in fits of cheer,
"Why are trees great friends? They always adhere!"
With every sapling that caught a wink,
They giggled and snickered, what did you think?

A bear rolled by with a chuckling grin,
"Why don't trees use phones? They can't keep in!"
The woodland echoed with each little jest,
Beneath the green canopy, each joke was the best!

Boughs of Banter

In the meadow, jokes take flight,
Branches swaying, what a sight!
A tree limb shared a clever pun,
While squirrels giggled, oh what fun!

Frogs leap in with witty rhymes,
Barking orders, calling chimes.
The oak rolls up its gnarled sleeves,
Spinning tales that no one believes!

Shrubs of Satire and Sass

Through the thickets, whispers course,
Bushes tease with merry force.
A rosebud cracks a snappy line,
While daisies dance, feeling fine!

The hedges giggle, oh so sly,
'We're rooting for you!' they reply.
With every joke, the laughter grows,
In the garden where humor flows!

Tree-mendous Tales of Tomfoolery

In the forest, roots entwine,
Laughter echoes, spirits shine.
A beech tree teases with a jest,
Spilling stories of the best!

The branches wave, a playful wave,
Tales of mischief, bold and brave.
As leaves engage in merry games,
The trunks high-five, sharing names!

The Lighthearted Ledger of Leafy Lore

In green pages, giggles sprout,
Each leaf holds a tale, no doubt.
Maples chuckle, while birches grin,
Every story invites a spin!

The ledger's thick with joy and glee,
Entries weave, as light dances free.
A pine interjects with a boast,
'I'm the tallest, raise a toast!'

Lighthearted Lingo Between the Stems

Among the leaves where laughter plays,
Squirrels chatter in funny ways.
Each acorn's joke is perfectly timed,
Nature's comedy, sweetly rhymed.

A raccoon winks, a clever tease,
As robins dance upon the breeze.
With every twig, a new pun grows,
In this grove where humor flows.

Beneath the bark, the laughter swells,
As in the branches, the mischief dwells.
A sapling whispers, 'I'm just a kid,'
While wise old oaks roll their eyes, I kid!

So gather round, hear every jest,
In this woodland where joy's expressed.
With every rustle, and giggle shared,
The forest's fun is always aired.

The Quipster's Quarters of Quercus

In the heart of Quercus, jokes take flight,
Where giggles blend with beams of light.
The branches sway, a pun parade,
With whispers of mirth, the shade is laid.

A jolly jay drops a quip or two,
While rabbits smile, hopping anew.
With every gust, a chuckle flows,
In Quercus' realm, the laughter grows.

Mushrooms pop with clever lines,
As ladybugs share secret signs.
Nature's wisecracks fill the air,
A playful banter beyond compare.

So let your heart be light and free,
Join the fun beneath the tree.
In Quercus' quarters, humor shines,
Where every leaf in laughter twines.

Mirthful Moments in the Moss

Upon the moss, where giggles sprout,
Laughter's echo dances about.
A toadstool hats a jester's crown,
In the forest, no one wears a frown.

The chipmunks tease with cheeky grins,
As light through branches softly spins.
"Life's a picnic!" croaks a wise old frog,
In this joyful, leafy dialogue.

The ferns sway with whimsy's tune,
Beneath the bright and cheerful moon.
Every creature plays their part,
In this woodland's joyful heart.

So step on soft and take your cue,
For mirthful moments wait for you.
Under green canopies of glee,
Find laughter stitched in nature's spree.

Foolish Footsteps Among the Firs

Among the firs where silliness grows,
Soft whispers weave through thickets close.
A pine cone roles, a clumsy fall,
As giggly spirits echo through all.

Sawdust showers, a playful rain,
As squirrels spin tales of joy and gain.
With every crunch of foliage near,
The breaths of laughter simply cheer.

A gnome nods with a twinkle bright,
Spreading fun from morn till night.
"Stay rooted in joy!" he seems to say,
As folly leads us on our way.

So dance along, oh merry friend,
In the firs where silly moments blend.
With footsteps light and hearts that soar,
Discover the fun forevermore.

Oaks of Outlandish Oddities

In a grove where shadows dance and play,
Trees wear smiles in their own quirky way.
One oak claimed to be a wise old sage,
But his jokes were just a little off-page.

A squirrel told tales of acorn affairs,
While tree bark giggled, shedding its cares.
The wind whistled jokes that made branches sway,
As laughter echoed through the brightening day.

The Seedling's Silly Secrets

Little seedlings sprouted without a care,
Whispering secrets to the bouncing air.
One claimed to sprout a crown of great gold,
But it was just a leaf that I was told!

They giggled at shadows that danced so bold,
Mapping out dreams in stories retold.
With laughter they grew, their roots intertwine,
In a world that's wacky, where they all shine.

Twisted Branches of Comedy

Branches twisted in the funniest ways,
Hosting a party for the sun's bright rays.
A jester squirrel played tricks with a nut,
While owls hooted jokes from their twilight rut.

Pine needles tickled the bark in delight,
As the stars above flickered in the night.
With each whispered laugh, the forest would glow,
Creating a show that nature would sow.

Lush Laughs in the Leaf Litter

In leaf litter lies a banquet of glee,
Where humor is sprouted and wild as the sea.
A worm wiggled in rhyme, making roots sway,
While crickets chirped jokes that brightened the day.

Among the ferns, chuckles erupted with zest,
As mushrooms exchanged wisecracks, feeling blessed.
Nature's comedy club under the trees,
Where laughter is boundless, flowing like breeze.

Bark and Banter Beneath the Sky

In the shade of trees we chat,
Squirrels roll their eyes at that.
Branches sway with laughter bright,
Nature's jesters take to flight.

Leaves whisper secrets in the breeze,
Ants march by with tiny ease.
Roots entwined in playful chat,
The forest floor, a mat of pat.

A raccoon jokes, a chipmunk grins,
Life is sweet where laughter begins.
Mushrooms giggle, shadows dance,
In this grove, we take a chance.

So gather round, both big and small,
Join the fun, we welcome all.
With every laugh, our hearts will mend,
In this grove, joy has no end.

Humorous Hues of the Hedge

The hedgehogs chuckle, spines in place,
With wrinkled snouts, they share their grace.
Colors bloom with jokes so bright,
Nature's palette, pure delight.

A leaf drops down to make a pun,
The sun shines down, it's all in fun.
Berries blush under playful sun,
Each giggle's sweeter than a bun.

Hilarity in every shade,
The ferns and flowers join the parade.
Dewdrops sparkle in the light,
Each joke shared, a pure delight.

So let us revel in laughter's glow,
As the hedges share what they know.
In every hue, a funny twist,
Let joy abound, it can't be missed.

Frivolities of the Forest Floor

Among the ferns, where giggles grow,
Mushrooms dance in a silent show.
Each pebble chuckles, each twig grins,
Laughter flows where adventure begins.

A ladybug spins, a beetle twirls,
They join in games of swirls and swirls.
Beneath the canopy, smiles abound,
Forest follies in rhythm found.

The stream hums softly, a jovial tune,
Reflecting bright rays of the afternoon.
Every ripple tells a jest,
Nature's humor is truly the best.

So come along, embrace the spree,
In this woodland, wild and free.
With every step, let laughter soar,
In the joys of the forest floor.

Joyful Jests Among the Junipers

Juniper branches sway and twine,
Whispers of laughter, so divine.
Breezes carry jokes in flight,
Under the stars, all feels right.

The owls hoot with clever plays,
As fireflies blink in funny ways.
Each shadow dances, each petal gleams,
Nature's laughter fuels our dreams.

Squirrels chatter, a playful crew,
Sharing tales of mischief too.
Junipers stand with arms spread wide,
Welcoming joy, like a family pride.

So gather here, where fun is found,
In this corner of joy unbound.
With every laugh and every cheer,
The spirit of mirth is always near.

Laugh Lines of the Lodgepole

In the woods where the lodgepoles stand,
Silly jokes grow like grains of sand.
With every whisper, a giggle or two,
Trees chuckle softly, it's all just for you.

Branches sway with a rhythmic glee,
Telling tales that tickle the knee.
Every rustle is laughter that spreads,
While squirrels roll over where sunshine treads.

Nature's comedy, a leafy delight,
As shadows dance in the shimmering light.
So gather 'round, let the laughter ignite,
In the heart of the grove, everything's bright.

With roots entwined, we'll tell our lore,
In the forest's embrace, who could ask for more?
A lodgepole's quip is worth its weight,
Come share a laugh, it's never too late.

The Cheery Chirp of the Chipper

Chirps and giggles in the bright sun's glow,
Chipper birds put on quite the show.
They flit and they flurry, with jokes to share,
Feathers ruffled in the light spring air.

One sings of twigs and another of seeds,
While above, the woodpecker's laughter leads.
Pine cones fall like the punchlines they throw,
In nature's stand-up, the humor's on show!

When pine needles titter, the forest will cheer,
With every sweet note, the smiles appear.
From branches to shrubs, the fun never ends,
Join in the laughter; the grove never pretends.

Under the canopy, where the sunshine streams,
The chirping chorus fulfills woodland dreams.
So listen closely to nature's own beat,
As the songs of the chipper bring joy to your feet.

Tickling the Trunks with Tales

Round the trunks where the shadows play,
Stories emerge in a whimsical way.
With every knot and twist, truth unfolds,
Whimsical fables that nature beholds.

Each bark bears witness to laughter and jest,
As critters convene for their evening fest.
A raccoon recounts his mischievous spree,
While owls hoot back in a wise parody.

Tickles of moss with tales in the breeze,
Crickets chirping as they tease the trees.
Whispers of humor through branches they send,
In the woodland theatre, where laughter won't end.

So pull up a stump, let the stories pour,
Each punchline a knot that we can explore.
With every bark's tale and every small laugh,
We find joy in the grove, nature's own craft.

Boisterous Breezes and Funny Faces

The breeze brings giggles that dance through the day,
Playing tricks on the pines in a merry ballet.
Faces in bark, oh what a sight!
Each one is grinning, what a pure delight!

Swirling the leaves into whimsical spins,
Nature's own jester where laughter begins.
Tickled by gusts, they sway with such grace,
Every turn brings more fun to this place.

With each tree's grin, the laughter grows wide,
Winking at passersby, with humor as guide.
A stand-up routine that never falls flat,
As breezes tickle, the fun is a fact!

So let's raise a cheer for the giggling wind,
For the jokes of the forest are never thinned.
With each swing and sway, we find our own space,
In the arms of the grove with its funny embrace.

Whispers Among the Pines

In the forest, trees do chat,
With a joke that makes you splat.
The branches sway, they giggle too,
Leaves falling down, a laugh anew.

Squirrels jest about their nuts,
While sparrows chirp, 'Don't pull the guts!'
The wind carries tales so spry,
In piney laughter, we all fly.

Mossy carpets hide surprise,
As each tree wears a funny disguise.
Bark-soft jokes in the gentle breeze,
Nature's humor brings us to our knees.

Dancing shadows hide and seek,
Every creak creates a cheeky peak.
Among the greens, the laughter grows,
In these woods, anything goes!

Cedar's Sassy Echo

Cedar's voice is sharp and clear,
Echoing sass, we all must cheer.
In every ring, a tale that's spun,
Come for the trees, stay for the pun!

Branches stretch like arms to play,
They tickle clouds and sway all day.
With every breeze, a witty remark,
It's a comedy show in the dark.

As critters laugh and share a smile,
Each bough's quip is worth your while.
Beneath the bark, there's humor true,
In cedar hugs, we all break through.

So lean in close, and hear the fun,
Nature's jesting has just begun.
Underneath the twisting vines,
We'd pine for more of these funny signs.

Spruce Yourself Up

If you feel low, just spruce up quick,
Like a tree adding a funny trick.
Branches feathery, always right,
In the sunlight, they shine so bright.

A little twist, a bend, a wig,
Spruce trees know how to dance a jig.
With every bounce, they teach us cheer,
Laughter's a bloom, let's hold it near.

Flicks of color, nature's grace,
In the forest, find your place.
Embrace the giggles that nature brings,
Spruce yourself up, it's time for flings!

So shake those needles, and laugh along,
Join the chorus, with nature's song.
In every bough, there's wittiness found,
Spruce you up, let joy abound!

Fir Real, It's Spring

The snowdrops peek, a season new,
Fir trees smile, with a sapling view.
In a world bursting, with colors bright,
They giggle softly, with delight.

As buds bloom, and children dash,
Every twig holds a hidden splash.
Nature's laughter is close at hand,
In this green kingdom, joy is planned.

The sun breaks through, a golden ray,
Sprigs of joy chase gloom away.
With every rustle, hear the cheer,
Fir real, it's spring, the time is here!

So pull on boots and tread the ground,
In every step, joy knows no bounds.
Let's take the paths where laughter rings,
Fir real, together, let's spread our wings!

Sarcasm Sprouts in the Saplings

In the shade of the tall, wise trees,
Saplings giggle in a playful breeze.
"I'm knotty, but I grow on you,"
Said the sage with branches, who always knew.

Beneath the barks, the laughter swings,
Each leaf a joke, as nature sings.
The squirrels snicker from the branches above,
With acorn caps, wearing hats made of love.

Raccoons in masks with a cheeky grin,
"Take a leaf, it's a great way to win!"
The forest floor dances in a punny spree,
As shadows chuckle at the wise old tree.

In this grove of giggles and glee,
Every trunk holds a tale to see.
With roots embedded in jest and cheer,
The heart of the forest whispers, "Stay near!"

Witty Whorls of the Wilderness

In swirls of leaves where the laughter peaks,
Critters trade quips in a language that speaks.
"I'm a bark-tender, mix me a drink!"
Said the moose with a wink, as they clink, clink, clink.

A bear in a bowtie, asking for honey,
Says, "Life is sweet; isn't that funny?"
With each flutter of wings from a chirpy throng,
"We're here for the jokes; we've all sung along!"

The owls on branches hoot with precision,
"Who's got the last word? It's our mission!"
Pinecones dropping with a thud and a thump,
"Let's roll with the jokes; give life a good pump!"

In this wildwood where hilarity flows,
Every creature knows that laughter grows.
With nature's punchlines, they leap and they spin,
In the whirl of the woods, the joy's found within.

Pine-sational Yarn-Spinning

Gather round, oh friends of the trees,
Let me spin you a tale in the soft, cool breeze.
Tall tales echoed through the pines,
Where humor wraps around like old vines.

A squirrel declared, with a nutty obsession,
"I'm simply nuts; it's my best profession!"
While the woodpecker tapped on a tree's wooden nose,
"Why do they call it a snap? That's just how it goes!"

In the twist of the ferns, a fox tells a joke,
"Why did the owl bring a book? To provoke!"
With a flip of his tail, and a gleeful shout,
The saplings erupt, no room for doubt!

So let's weave this yarn; let's spin it right,
Through laughter-laden paths, we'll dance in delight.
With every tall tale and every good pun,
Life's a grand story—a joke just begun!

Humor in the Hollow of Hearts

In the meadow where merry-time bloomed,
Laughter echoed, no room for gloom.
A tree with a grin, its branches outspread,
"Why do trees get sick? Because they need bed!"

Bunnies chuckle while skipping in pairs,
"Don't be so 'hare'-brained, let down your cares!"
With each little hop, a chuckle to share,
These woods brim with love; oh, what a flair!

A hedge hog rolled up, with a snicker so bright,
"Life's prickly at times, but don't lose your light."
The whispers of nature blend joy and mirth,
In this cozy hollow, there's too much worth.

So gather your friends, let the laughter start,
For joy blooms deeper in the hollow of hearts.
With every chuckle and smile that we lend,
The spirit of humor will never end!

Canopy of Cleverness

In the woods where trees tickle high,
Squirrels chuckle and giggles fly.
Branches sway with playful glee,
Nature's jesters, wild and free.

Leaves whisper secrets, soft and light,
Beneath the boughs, the jokes take flight.
Twigs dance around like they know the score,
In this leafy realm, there's always more.

Roots that revolutionize quite the art,
Gnarled and knotted with a twisty heart.
Bark becomes the punchline of the day,
Nature's grin in a charming display.

Mushrooms giggle at the passing breeze,
Spouting humor with such perfect ease.
In this lush domain where laughter grows,
Every nook and cranny knows how it goes.

Nature's Quirky Quips

In vibrant fields where daisies wink,
The wind shares secrets quicker than you think.
Frogs croak rhythms, a comedic tune,
Even the sun can't help but swoon.

Sassy squirrels with bushy tails,
Make nutty jokes about their epic fails.
Every acorn holds a story bold,
In jest and joy, the truth unfolds.

Buzzing bees with their dance so bright,
Pollinate laughter from day to night.
Every flower sways to a clever beat,
Nature's humor is truly sweet.

Rabbits spin tales, oh so sly,
While birds compose limericks up high.
In this playful glade, all is well,
Whispers of whimsy cast a spell.

Verdant Verses of Vexation

Amidst the greens where the weeds tease,
Bumblebees argue over whose buzz is a breeze.
Knotty branches twist and bend,
In this tangled tale, there's laughter without end.

Thorns throw shade with a prickly jest,
Even the thistles try their best.
Every blade of grass, a comic flare,
Sprouting humor with the freshest air.

Fallen leaves gossip of summer's faux pas,
Watching the seasons with a giggling aha!
Nature's canvas splashed with mirth,
Each droplet of dew holding laughter's birth.

In the shade where shadows play,
The forest chuckles at the light of day.
With every rustle and swaying limb,
The laughter of flora remains never dim.

Pine-scented Punchlines

Underneath the canopy of gnarled pine,
The stout trunk leans, it found the right line.
With whispers lingering in the cool air,
Laughter echoes, everywhere.

Woodpeckers tap out a clever beat,
As chipmunks dance on their tiny feet.
Pinecones roll with a giggly spin,
In this leafy stage, where fun's always in.

The sun beams down with a radiant grin,
Even the clouds join in on the fun within.
Nature's remarks, sharp and spry,
In this realm, humor can never die.

Rascally rabbits hop with delight,
As nature's jokes take flight.
With every breeze, it's clear to see,
The forest laughs in harmony.

Shade of Wit

Under branches vast and wide,
The laughter echoing inside.
With jokes that twist and turn around,
In the shade, my joy is found.

A squirrel stirs with a cheeky grin,
Cracking jokes as he scurries in.
"Why did the tree go to school?"
"Because it wanted to be more cool!"

A breeze chuckles through the leaves,
Sharing tales that no one believes.
"Did you hear about the pine cone's fate?
It fell in love—it was first-rate!"

So gather near, embrace the mirth,
For humor thrives upon this earth.
With every giggle, joy takes flight,
In the shade, everything feels right.

Twisted Oaks and Silly Jokes

In the forest where laughter grows,
Twisted oaks tell jokes, who knows?
"Why was the tree afraid of heights?
Because it couldn't handle the flights!"

Underneath the canopy so green,
Nature's punchline can be seen.
"When does a tree become a musician?
When it's in perfect pitch—what a transition!"

The mossy floor feels like a stage,
Where jokes unfold, turning every page.
"My bark is worse than my bite!" they chime,
In twisted tales, they spin in rhyme.

So come and let your worries fade,
Where laughter grows in leafy shade.
Silly jokes and smiles declare,
In this grove, there's joy to share.

Pine-Scented Wordplay

Amidst the needles, sharp and bright,
The air is filled with pure delight.
"Why did the sapling break up, just so?
It found its roots, but couldn't grow!"

The pine-scented breeze carries a jest,
In this grove, we feel so blessed.
"How do trees learn their ABCs?
They branch out with the greatest of ease!"

Laughter dapples through the green,
With every quip, a lovely scene.
"Why did the tree become a banker?
To branch out and be a major stanker!"

So join me here in nature's play,
Where humor thrives in a leafy way.
Pine-scented giggles fill the air,
A joyful heart is ours to share.

A Sprightly Needled Nonsense

In a grove where laughter leads,
Sprightly nonsense plants its seeds.
"What did the tree say to the stump?
I'm rooting for you, give it a jump!"

With needles dancing all around,
Silliness is the sweetest sound.
"Why don't trees use computers?
Because they fear the 'byte' in their tutors!"

The sunlight giggles, shadows play,
With every quirk, we laugh away.
"Did you hear about the forest race?
The trees all took their time, just to embrace!"

So come and join this merry spree,
Where joylight reigns, and we feel free.
In sprightly nonsense, smiles abound,
In every corner of this ground.

Sappy Attempts at Humor

In the forest, trees do schmooze,
Their bark is worse than their news.
Saplings giggle, branches sway,
Leafy laughter's here to play.

Knots and twists in every joke,
A log's life isn't just a poke.
When pine trees crack a grin,
You know the fun is about to begin.

Nature's punchlines hit like rain,
With every drop, a new refrain.
Branches waving to the punch,
Forest humor packs a crunch!

So let's log in for a cheer,
For tree-mendous jokes, lend your ear.
With every thought, a new sap flows,
In these woods, the humor grows!

Understory of Sarcasm

Under the boughs, whispers quip,
The sarcasm takes a dip.
Roots entwined in witty banter,
Hidden gems that make us chanter.

Branches shrug at passing deer,
"Hey buddy, do you even steer?"
Witty leaves in quizzical flair,
Sarcastic vibes fill the air.

Trees with attitude on full show,
"Stop leafing, stay here, don't go!"
Twisted vines, they clearly state,
"Don't branch out, just celebrate!"

In the shade, humor lingers close,
"Keep it rooted," is what they boast.
With every rustle, a chuckle's born,
In nature's snark, we're never worn!

Roots of Riddles

Down below where secrets hide,
Roots of riddles twist and glide.
"Why do trees get chill in spring?"
"Because they wait for warmth to cling!"

In the soil, thoughts take form,
Trunk-tales twist outside the norm.
"Why did the seed sit in the shade?"
"Too much sun, it quickly frayed!"

Beneath the earth where quips reside,
"Why's the tree so calm and wide?"
"Because it's great at letting go,
And waving branches in the flow!"

Crafting riddles in the dark,
These roots? They leave a happy mark.
Every puzzle's bound to stump,
In this grove, we rise, then jump!

Canopy of Crack-Ups

High above, the laughter soars,
Branches bending as humor pours.
"Why do squirrels always win?
They've got the nuts to throw and spin!"

Leaves shake with glee, what a sight,
Giggling shadows dance in light.
"Why did the crow sit on the tree?
To try out for a birdie spree!"

Woodpeckers drum a merry beat,
As each joke lands, it's quite the feat.
"Why do trees always get in line?
They know the root of having a good time!"

Under the canopy, joy ignites,
With every chuckle, day ignites.
Nature's comedy fills the air,
In this grove, everyone's a player!

Forest Frolics and Playful Tales

In the woods where laughter sings,
The squirrels dance on tiny swings.
The owl hoots with a twinkling eye,
As frogs leap by, oh my, oh my!

The trees whisper jokes in rustling leaves,
While the rabbit plots on what it weaves.
"Why did the twig not branch out?" they'll say,
"Because it found its roots too hard to sway!"

A chattering chipmunk starts a race,
With acorn helmets, they pick up pace.
"Stop leafing around!" the woodpecker cries,
As laughter echoes through the skies!

By the brook, the turtles make a bet,
"Who can outgrin without a sweat?"
They chuckle and splash, it's quite the scene,
Even the fish join in, so serene!

Sprig of Humor Under the Canopy

Beneath the boughs where shadows play,
The mischievous gnomes like to stay.
"Let's leaf this place and branch out wide,
Or do we stay and enjoy the ride?"

A wise old turtle shared a fable,
About a fruit that grew quite unstable.
"Why did the apple break the mold?
It wanted to be the core of the bold!"

The raccoons gather with snacks to munch,
Trading tall tales over their lunch.
"Why did the pine tree feel so blue?
Because the spruce said it couldn't stick too!"

As evening falls, the fireflies glow,
Casting light on each pun-filled show.
With giggles and grins, the night takes flight,
In this forest of jest, all feels just right!

The Quirky Quirk of Quercus

In oak's embrace, the giggles bloom,
Where every acorn holds a room.
"What's a tree's favorite drink?" they tease,
"Root beer, of course, it's sure to please!"

The winding vines entwine in jest,
While critters gather for a little fest.
"Why was the birch so good at math?
It knew how to calculate its path!"

Bouncing bugs let laughter spring,
As the playful breeze starts to sing.
"Why did the twig get in a fight?
It was tired of being bent just right!"

Amidst the trees, the stories flow,
With a quirky twist, they steal the show.
So join the fun beneath the shade,
Where every folly is happily made!

Sapling Smiles in the Shade

In the grove where young ones sprout,
The laughter's loud, without a doubt.
"Why did the seed start to prance?
It knew it had a chance to dance!"

The dappled light winks through the lea,
As critters gather, wild and free.
"Why do roots stick together tight?
They're bound by love, what a sight!"

Bright blossoms giggle in the sun,
While playful breezes help them run.
"Why was the grass always smiling?
Because it knew it was worth styling!"

As twilight paints the sky in gold,
These sapling smiles are stories told.
In whispering woods where joy won't fade,
We gather cheer, the memories made!

Droll Stories from the Dappled Light

In the shade where shadows play,
A squirrel shares a cheesy day.
Acorns roll like laughter's sound,
Nature's jokes are all around.

The owl hoots with a clever twist,
While rabbits dance, they can't resist.
A pinecone falls, the punchline drops,
And giggles echo, never stops.

The breeze carries a friendly jest,
As birds in chorus pass the test.
Their chirps are quips, a light-hearted thrill,
Among the trees, you get your fill.

In dappled light, the tales unfold,
Of silly slips and jokes retold.
So grab a seat on mossy ground,
In this green realm, humor's found.

The Spruce Spotlight on Savory Stories

In a clearing, under spruce so grand,
Lies a feast too good to withstand.
Berries whisper secrets sweet,
While ants march to a rhythmic beat.

A raccoon with a cookie grin,
Hides his snacks, but we all know when.
The pies they bake have crusts so fine,
Each slice tells a story, divine.

Spruce needles chuckle, a fragrant cheer,
As thistle thorns say, 'Have no fear!'
Laughter cooks in the simmering air,
In stories shared with playful flair.

Every moment a savory bite,
Flavor and fun, oh what delight!
In this spotlight, tales unfold,
Of tastiness and humor bold.

Heartfelt Humor in the Underbrush

Beneath the brush, where critters dwell,
A hedgehog spins a comical tale.
With spikes like quills, he tells his plight,
Of pranks gone wrong in the moonlight.

The chipmunks giggle at his clumsy spins,
While dance-offs start with laughter wins.
Even the fox joins in on the jest,
In underbrush, it's humor's nest.

A turtle, slow with a mime's finesse,
Shares wisdom wrapped in humor's dress.
Each giggle a reminder bright,
That joy is found in laughter's light.

So gather close where stories blend,
Hear heartful laughs that never end.
In leafy lanes, let spirits rise,
With humor's warmth, the heart complies.

The Jocular Juniper's Journal

In the grove, the juniper writes,
With berries bold, he shares his sites.
Every branch reflects a jest,
Crafting tales that simply zest.

A skit on squirrels with nutty schemes,
Caterpillars form their own dream teams.
In soft whispers, the leaves will cheer,
As tales unfold that keep us near.

Each entry, a laugh, a giggle, a glee,
Juniper's charm flows wild and free.
With every twig, a punchline flows,
Under the sun, the humor grows.

So turn the page where fun aligns,
In the journal where the laughter shines.
Jocular moments, both wise and new,
In the circle of life, joy's the view.

The Barking Comedian

In the grove where laughter grows,
A tree with jokes in every pose.
Its trunk is thick, its humor wide,
Leaves rustle with laughter, can't be denied.

Tapping on bark, the woodpecker sings,
Knocking on doors of punchlines and flings.
Roots in the soil, but reaching for jokes,
Funny as squirrels in their playful pokes.

Branches sway with a chuckle or two,
Every twig has a tale that's brand new.
The canopy giggles with each gentle breeze,
Life in the forest is certain to please.

Fallen branches can't hold their cheer,
Each one whispers a joke in your ear.
In this woods, laughter is more than a trend,
The bark's got the best, come gather, my friend!

Branching Out in Jest

High up in the branches, shenanigans unfold,
Each leaf tells a tale, some silly, some bold.
The laughter cascades like a waterfall bright,
Under the canopy, everything feels light.

A squirrel's acrobatics make everyone grin,
Diving through branches, where nonsense begins.
Bouncing on twigs, they leap and they play,
Telling tall tales of a bright sunny day.

The limbs stretch wide with their own brand of fun,
Tickling the sun as it dances and runs.
Jokes drift on breezes, from pine to the oak,
In the heart of the woods, punchlines provoke.

From roots to the leaves, laughter spreads like the dew,
Nature's own comedy, just waiting for you.
So swing on the branches, embrace all the jest,
In the land of the trees, we're all truly blessed!

Woodland Whimsy

In a forest of giggles, where shadows play tricks,
The trees have a humor that always still clicks.
Every rustle and creak is a quip or a pun,
Woodland whimsy laughs, it's all just good fun.

A bear tells a joke while chewing on bark,
"When it comes to my friends, I'm the king of the park!"
The rabbits hop by, with a bounce in their step,
Each thump on the ground is a punchline prepped.

Even the owls, wise as can be,
Chime in at dusk with a hoot full of glee.
Life in the woodland is never too tame,
With buddy trees teasing, we're all in the game.

So come take a stroll down this hoot-happy lane,
Where laughter is endless, and no one feels pain.
In this enchanted grove, humor's a breeze,
Join hands with a tree; let's just be at ease!

Snappy Saplings

Little saplings sprout with a giggly facade,
Tickling the soil, playing games with the sod.
Images of mischief dance in their heads,
As they tease the tall trees from their leafy beds.

"Hey, look at me! I'm growing so fast!"
They shout to the oaks, accounting their blast.
The tallest tree chuckles, its branches a sway,
"Stay low to the ground, you'll find humor pays!"

With whispers of jokes flowing through every leaf,
And trunks bending low, sharing scoffs of belief.
Playing tag with the shadows, they twist and they bend,
In the world of the forest, no sapling pretend.

So laugh with the younglings, so vibrant and spry,
Their capers in sunlight will spark a bright sky.
Nature's joke shop is well-stocked and bright,
With snappy little saplings bringing pure delight!

www.ingramcontent.com/pod-product-compliance
Lightning Source LLC
Chambersburg PA
CBHW071829160426
43209CB00003B/248